Glory to God Everywhere You Are There

I0191168

Lawson Hanson

Note: Unless otherwise specified the cited Bible text references are extracts from the KJV (King James Version, circa 1611) with updated more modern spelling.

Dedication

Glory to God Everywhere You Are There

Glory to God in the heavens,
Glory to God in the earth,
Glory to God Everywhere You Are There,
Glory to God's universe.

We praise You because You're Almighty,
We praise You because You're The One,
We praise You because You have
    saved us from sin,
By the sacrifice of Your own Son.

We worship the God of Creation,
We worship the Saviour Your Son, Jesus Christ,
We worship the Spirit You poured out on us,
And we worship all Three just as One.

You care for and You heal all we pray for,
You distribute Your Mercy and everlasting Grace,
You broadcast Your Love overflowing on us,
And protect us within Your embrace.

— Lawson Hanson, 5/3/2015, 15/4/2025.

Contents

Chapter 1

The Backstory

This document contains the lyrics and music score for a song which at first got called *"Glory To God"* — short, sharp and to the point.

After a decade of singing this as part of my prayers to Almighty God, I have renamed it to use a longer title: *"Glory To God Everywhere You are There."*

Why? Because I have re-worked the lyrics to make them more direct by using the second person pronoun *"You"* in place of the third person pronouns *"He,"* *"Him"* and *"His."*

In this song I want to communicate with and talk *to* God in a direct sense instead of talking *about* Him. I want to give my worship and heartfelt praises to God.

Yes, we should take every opportunity to talk *about* God. We can share our testimony with whomever will listen. We do that.

I composed this song during a time when I was coping with a serious health issue in my life. For me the lyrics of this simple song are exceeding precious.

God is not untouchable — God is right beside us no matter

where we go.

In the text below I provide a bit of background information.

My life as a *"born again"* Christian commenced when I was 25 years old.

A student who was completing his Ph.D work at the University of Melbourne told me about his own *"born again"* experience.

He told me about his miracle working God. People at his church got healed all the time through the power of faith in their prayers.

To say I got intrigued is an understatement.

He told me how Jesus preached the need to get *"born again"* when He spoke to a man named Nicodemus:

> 1. *There was a man of the Pharisees, named Nicodemus, a ruler of the Jews:*
> 2. *The same came to Jesus by night, and said unto him, Rabbi, we know that thou art a teacher come from God: for no man can do these miracles that thou doest, except God be with him.*
> 3. *Jesus answered and said unto him, Verily, verily, I say unto thee, Except a man be born again, he cannot see the kingdom of God.*
> 4. *Nicodemus saith unto him, How can a man be born when he is old? can he enter the second time into his mother's womb, and be born?*
> 5. *Jesus answered, Verily, verily, I say unto thee, Except a man be born of water and of the Spirit, he cannot enter into the kingdom of God.*
> 6. *That which is born of the flesh is flesh; and that which is born of the Spirit is spirit.*
> 7. *Marvel not that I said unto thee, Ye must be born again.*
> — John 3:1–7

Nicodemus struggled to understand the imperative statement *"Ye must be born again."*

Another vital piece of information gets provided for us in the opening verses of the book of Acts:

> 1. *The former treatise have I made, O Theophilus, of all that Jesus began both to do and teach,*
> 2. *Until the day in which he was taken up, after that he through the Holy Ghost had given commandments unto the apostles whom he had chosen:*
> 3. *To whom also he shewed himself alive after his passion by many infallible proofs, being seen of them forty days, and speaking of the things pertaining to the kingdom of God:*
> 4. *And, being assembled together with them, commanded them that they should not depart from Jerusalem, but wait for the promise of the Father, which, saith he, ye have heard of me.*
> 5. *For John truly baptized with water; but ye shall be baptized with the Holy Ghost not many days hence.*
> — Acts 1:1–5

Look especially at the words in verses 4 and 5.

Jesus commanded His disciples to *"wait"* in Jerusalem for what He called *"the promise of the Father."*

The disciples did what Jesus commanded and as a result of that they each received their own experience of getting *"baptized with the Holy Ghost not many days hence"*:

> 1. *And when the day of Pentecost was fully come, they were all with one accord in one place.*

2. And suddenly there came a sound from heaven as of a rushing mighty wind, and it filled all the house where they were sitting.
3. And there appeared unto them cloven tongues like as of fire, and it sat upon each of them.
4. And they were all filled with the Holy Ghost, and began to speak with other tongues, as the Spirit gave them utterance.
— Acts 2:1–4

The infilling of the Holy Ghost is always accompanied by God giving us the ability *"to speak with other tongues."*

This noisy event drew a great crowd of people to investigate what was going on. Peter the apostle stood up to address the crowd. Here is a part of what he said as recorded for us:

36. Therefore let all the house of Israel know assuredly, that God hath made the same Jesus, whom ye have crucified, both Lord and Christ.
37. Now when they heard this, they were pricked in their heart, and said unto Peter and to the rest of the apostles, Men and brethren, what shall we do?
38. Then Peter said unto them, Repent, and be baptized every one of you in the name of Jesus Christ for the remission of sins, and ye shall receive the gift of the Holy Ghost.
39. For the promise is unto you, and to your children, and to all that are afar off, even as many as the LORD our God shall call.
— Acts 2:36–39

Martin, the Ph.D student who shared this good news with me was adamant that this is the key. This is the truth for which we have all been searching.

I needed to follow Peter's advice:

"Repent, and be baptized every one of you in the name of Jesus Christ for the remission of sins, and ye shall receive the gift of the Holy Ghost."

After five or six months I accepted one of his invitations to attend a meeting at the church he went to. I am so glad I did.

It felt as if I was coming home! It's a happy place with a sea of genuine smiling faces. This church has centres scattered across the world. Australia, New Zealand, Papua New Guinea, Fiji, Africa, Italy, England, Poland, Canada and more. You can find out much more at this link:

https://www.revivalcentres.org

I got baptized after my second meeting. For the first time in over a decade I felt as if I had taken a step in the *right* direction — towards God instead of always moving the other way.

Five weeks after I got baptized, in the manner that John the Baptist used, by *complete* immersion in water, I received my own *"day of Pentecost"* experience.

It took me five weeks to sort out my thinking and to understand what my repentance meant. It needs a complete change of mind — I was a bit slow.

One morning I was praying in a quiet voice at home. I was thanking God for the delightful changes He had helped to bring about in my life in a matter of weeks.

Through simple prayers offered for me or by me I had stopped smoking, stopped drinking alcohol and had a long-standing pain in my nose healed. Each of those happened in an instant or over night. I noticed my speech contained far less expletives.

As I was praying there came a change when I received the gift of the Holy Spirit. I was speaking in other tongues as the Spirit gave me the utterance. My speech was quiet and clear, yet no longer my natural tongue.

These new words streamed out of my mouth. There was no extraordinary effort required.

I could stop the praying in tongues and I could start praying in tongues again. I was in complete control of this wonderful gift that God had graciously bestowed upon me.

In an instant of time, on the 27th July, 1975, I knew for certain that God is real and that He loves me more than I can imagine. There's One God who *can* answer our call. He says He will and He honours His Word.

This audible gift gives us a personal prayer language that gets used for our direct communication with Almighty God. It's a precious gift that He expects us to use every day. It brings great benefits including peace and comfort and joy. It provides Spiritual insight into the kingdom of God.

Later that year I met my wife Heather in the church and together with The Lord, we feel blessed to receive the excellent teaching about God and His ways, that we do in our church.

For the next 38 years I lived my life in the knowledge that God is alive and that He cares for us and I know Him as my closest friend — the heavenly Father. God hears and answers our calls to Him and I know Him as a miracle working God.

My life was and still is happy and joyful — better than I ever imagined it could be.

That does not mean it has been without incident that has needed us to press in and seek the Lord with sincere diligence to help us get through our difficulties.

There came a time when I needed to learn a lesson in life.

Receiving the gift of the Holy Spirit does not automatically make us immune to the results of our own stupidity.

Please read that sentence again.

My eating habits got out of control.

I was working long hours, and started drinking too many cups of sweetened coffee as well as consuming caffeine and sugar-laden carbonated drinks every day. I needed these to help me stay alert.

It did not take long before an annual checkup with my GP determined that my blood glucose levels were far too high and I had developed diabetes type-2. I needed to start taking medications to help keep my blood glucose levels down.

The prescribed medicines left me feeling awful. This was my fault, because instead of trying to curb my intake of high sugar content and carbohydrate foods, I kept eating fast food and drinking fizzy drinks like they were going out of fashion, as I had been for more years than I could remember.

At my heaviest, I weighed in at 105 kilograms. That is: 16.5 stone, or 231 pounds. My BMI was 36.3.

Although BMI is no longer considered a perfect indicator of our health it's still a reasonable guide.

A normal BMI should fall in the range from 18.5 to 24.9 and by that standard — I was far beyond obese.

I started to mismanage my diabetes type-2, often skipping the medications because of the way these made me feel.

I didn't realise what serious damage I was doing to my health.

In 2013, one morning after I had travelled into my place of work in the city about an hour's train ride from my outer-suburban home I felt decidedly unwell. Unbeknown to me I was experiencing an *Ischaemic* Stroke episode.

I apologised to my supervisor saying I was feeling very sick and I was going home. He tried to call an ambulance for me. I refused saying *"I'm heading home."* Yes I know I can be a stubborn old coot.

I travelled home again crawled into bed and stayed there for the rest of that day and night. My wife, Heather, tried to coax me out to eat our evening meal and I refused saying *"I need to get more sleep."*

In the morning of the next day I found that I could not move the limbs on the left side of my body. My left arm did not obey the *"Up"* command and my left leg could not support my weight when I attempted to stand.

Heather rushed me off to see our GP and he ordered me straight into hospital. After two or three days in the Stroke Ward undergoing lots of medical scans and other tests the results of these determined that my stroke got caused by a blocked artery near the base of my brain on the right side of my head.

Because of my long delay in getting to hospital a lot of brain cells had already died — starved of oxygenated blood supply — and soon I got transferred to a Rehabilitation Hospital.

We got told I should expect to spend the next six months there and would be most likely to go home in a wheel chair or at best with a supportive walking frame.

I struggle to find words to adequately describe how weird it is to wake up and find your limbs have gone on a relaxing holiday without you. They sat there motionless not listening to a single demand I gave them for action.

I was unable to lift or move either my left arm or my left leg. Try as I may they would not move. Apart from the lack of mobility, other difficulties included impaired speech, and my head felt like a *"fuzz ball."*

Thinking in a straight line was most difficult.

As Heather and I gradually digested this information from the medical team, together in quiet tones we earnestly prayed to God, calling upon the wonderful name of Jesus our Saviour, asking for their miracle working power in my life.

When visiting hours were over, Heather needed to leave. We said our tearful *"Goodbyes,"* knowing that I was in a good place that could provide the best of man's medical care for me. All the medical staff we met were exceptional individuals who always gave their utmost ability to care for me.

After I had eaten a small *"right hand only"* dinner, and before I settled down to sleep for the night, I reminded myself that I was a born again child of God.

Despite my *"fuzz ball"* brain fog I reminded myself that *"God created everything."* I knew *"with God all things are possible."* I knew *"Jesus healed all that were sick."* I knew our call to Almighty God gets heard and I knew our hope and expectation was for God to heal me.

Soon after my meditative prayer and as I was resting on my bed, my left leg straightened and my left foot turned; almost in slow motion, all by itself, no intention or effort from me.

"Is that you Lord?" I asked in my mind. Again, my left leg straightened and my left foot turned. *"I'll take that as a yes!"* I said inside myself. Again, my left leg straightened and my left foot turned. I smiled and thanked my God for His never ending mercy.

This gentle manipulation of my left leg extending and the slight foot rotation continued, four or five times each minute. In my mind I wondered and then asked the Lord: *"Should I resist these actions or should I relax?"*

In an instant the leg manipulation stopped and everything was quiet and calm.

After a moment or two I realised *"Oh! How silly of me."* *"That was a double question!"* *"I'll try them one at a time."*

So I asked: *"Should I resist what You are doing?"* Still everything remained quiet.

Next I asked: *"Should I relax and let You do what You do?"* In an instant my left leg straightened out and my left foot turned in those two gentle motions. *"I'll take that as a Yes,"* I concluded.

The motion of left leg straightening with the left foot turning continued to happen about a hundred times before I drifted off to a peaceful and sound sleep. I expect you have heard of *"counting sheep ..."*

The following morning I found that I had enough strength in my right side to heave myself up on the side of the bed and I was then able to lift myself so that I could actually stand for one or two moments.

Then I made a slow, unstoppable, slip back down and crumpled onto the floor. I had not thought about what I was doing and falling toward my left side I had nothing close by to grab with my stronger right hand.

Within moments the door flew open and nurses rushed in to help me back up and onto the bed again. I had triggered a motion sensor!

Later that day I started a long series of rehabilitation sessions. During a simple physiotherapy assessment, I found that I was able to raise my left leg, about five millimetres, for about five seconds. That was more than I had managed to achieve for four or five days before.

For two or three weeks, day after day, each night in my bed, the gentle leg and foot manipulations continued, and the following day I found that I was able to achieve more than I had been able to do the day before.

There were dozens of different therapy sessions; some to explore speech, some for cognitive thinking, others for eyesight and vision, and there were sessions to help me learn how to walk again and sessions to design orthotic inserts for my shoes to help me walk with more stability. Other sessions gave practical advice to prepare stroke patients to help us integrate back into a new form of post-stroke life.

My sincere thanks go to the teams of professional medical people who each had a hand in my recovery. Without them that process would have been more difficult, and I thank them all for their extraordinary care.

Over and above these professional medical facilities, I give continual praise to God in Whom I believe. I praise Him for creating people with the patience and ability to provide the wonderful care that they do.

With each passing day I was becoming more able to move both limbs on the left side of my body. Tentative and gradual at first and by small degree, then with much practise, there came a day when I could *raise* my left arm *over* my head! Jubilation! I gave praise and thanks to my God.

A brother in the Lord had come in to visit me on that day and he noticed the physiotherapist had written *"FROM"* on my patient worksheet. He asked what that meant and we got told: *"Full Range of Movement."* We both rejoiced in the Lord on hearing that great news.

Over time, I soon progressed from a wheel chair to a high walking frame, and then on to a low walking frame, then a pair of crutches, and then managed to start walking with a single *"walking stick."* It was slow; it was awkward; it was progress.

At last, six (6) *weeks* (not months) after I had arrived there, I got permitted to go home for a part-day visit, to let me see if I could navigate steps and the other features at our house.

Returning to the rehabilitation hospital to complete more physiotherapy sessions, I was soon permitted to leave, and resume living at home full time. At last, life was starting to get back to a new form of normal.

I thoroughly praise God for the healing He provided. The gradual nature of the healing process gave me more opportunity to say: *"Thank You Lord,"* and I got more amazed at what His wonderful creation we call the human body involves. *"The hip bone's connected to the ..."*

I was able to thank and praise God for every day, and for each advancement that He provided as I came to appreciate more about how miraculous is our design, and how wonderfully are we made. Our God is brilliant and gracious and most merciful.

I had been living life, going through the motions, taking too much for granted without remembering to praise and glorify God for all that He does for us every moment of the day.

Have you ever driven your motor vehicle from point A to point B and then wondered *"How did I get here?"* *"I do not remember coming through the intersections at X and Y, or Z!"* Rather alarming and perplexing.

I am thankful that this does not happen every day. I can remember at least one such instance. It's better to pay attention to what we are doing and *"park"* the other thoughts that can impinge on our thinking until such a time as we can devote time to that without possible impact on others.

God looks after us a whole lot more than that for which we give Him credit.

The Bible reminds us with words like these:

> 29. *Give unto the LORD the glory due unto his name: bring an offering, and come before him: worship the LORD in the beauty of holiness.*

. . .

34. *O give thanks unto the LORD; for he is good;*
for his mercy endureth for ever.
— 1 Chronicles 16:29 and 34

Two years later, in 2015, I needed to undergo CABG (Coronary Artery Bypass Graft) *heart surgery* for a triple bypass.

My out of control eating habits had also caused a narrowing of the arteries in my heart and when I found I was continually feeling *"out of breath"* a referral to a Cardiac specialist determined these blocked arteries needed urgent repair.

Although considered a *standard* procedure these days there are moments when your heart gets cooled down to stop it beating while the medical team goes about the tasks of making extensive precision sutured repairs to the grafts used to bypass the affected areas.

When the surgery nears completion the surgeons disconnect the heart-lung machine that has been helping to keep you alive and begin to warm up your heart until *"all by itself"* it commences beating again and the healing and recovery process begins to make progress at an almost alarming rate.

I was out of hospital within five or six days. They had soon removed all the sutures from my chest and from my left arm and my right leg where they had extracted parts of my veins for use in making the necessary bypasses.

I got sent home with strong pain killers that I did not need to take after the dose they gave me before I went home. I thank my God for taking away all the pain.

Instances of personal experiences like these two episodes has caused me to reflect deeply about the wonderful nature of our human bodies and to give all the praise and glory to our mighty and gracious God of Creation.

The genesis of the words for my song started at about that

time. A near brush with death can make us sit up and take stock of life and be ever so thankful to Almighty God Who gave us such a precious gift.

My belief in God stems from the personal experience of receiving the gift of the Holy Spirit with the accompanying evidence of speaking in other *unlearned* tongues.

Jesus says we *"must* be *born again."*

Jesus used this *imperative* statement to describe why this is necessary:

> 24. *God is a Spirit: and they that worship him must worship him in spirit and in truth.*
> — John 4:24

What does that mean? *God is a Spirit?* And to worship Him we *"must worship him in spirit and in truth."*

We ourselves are part flesh and blood body and we are part human *"spirit."*

In the book of Ecclesiastes we can read:

> 20. *All go unto one place; all are of the dust, and all turn to dust again.*
> — Ecclesiastes 3:20

Our flesh and blood body gets created from the dust or the elements of the earth. When we die our mortal body will then decay and get reduced again to *"dust."*

> 7. *Then shall the dust return to the earth as it was: and the spirit shall return unto God who gave it.*
> — Ecclesiastes 12:7

The *"spirit"* is the part of us that distinguishes whether we are alive or dead. When we die our *spirit* departs from our physical deceased body location and returns *"to God who gave it."*

What *must* we do to enable us to worship God both *"in spirit"* and *"in truth?"*

In the first book of Corinthians, it's explained that *when* we pray in *unknown tongues*, this is when our *spirit prays*:

> 14. *For if I pray in an unknown tongue, my spirit prayeth, but my understanding is unfruitful.*
> — 1 Corinthians 14:14

The initial outpouring of God's Holy Spirit on the day of Pentecost about 2,000 years ago got extended, *that same day,* to over 3,000 people.

Since then, this experience has been available to anyone who will call out to God, on His terms: truly *"repentant"* and in obedience, getting *"baptised"* — *"in the name of Jesus Christ for the remission of sins."*

Almighty God of All Creation has these words to say to us:

> 11. *For I know the thoughts that I think toward you, saith the LORD, thoughts of peace, and not of evil, to give you an expected end.*
> 12. *Then shall ye call upon me, and ye shall go and pray unto me, and I will hearken unto you.*
> 13. *And ye shall seek me, and find me, when ye shall search for me with all your heart.*
> — Jeremiah 29:11–13

Look at these verses — God expects us to *"call upon"* Him and to *"pray unto"* Him. When we do this He promises *"I will hearken unto you."*

God expects us to *"seek"* for Him in a circumspect manner and says we will *"find"* Him when we *"search for"* God *"with all our heart."*

When we approach God in this way He says with certainty we *"shall"* — He guarantees we will — *"find"* Him.

Like the Psalmist says we need to be honest with God:

> 23. *Search me, O God, and know my heart: try me, and know my thoughts:*
> 24. *And see if there be any wicked way in me, and lead me in the way everlasting.*
> — Psalms 139:23–24

It's impossible to *"fool"* God.

Our repentance needs to be *"from the heart."*

By the Grace of God, He subsequently fills us with His gift of the Holy Spirit; and we speak out in other tongues, as He has promised we will.

From that moment onwards, we know that God is there. He is alive and well and we have made direct contact with Him.

God wants us to communicate with Him:

> 3. *Call unto me, and I will answer thee, and shew thee great and mighty things, which thou knowest not.*
> — Jeremiah 33:3

I can speak in other tongues whenever I choose, knowing that my personal communication gets heard and understood by the Almighty God of Creation. The veracity of this experience has never left me, and becomes more precious every day.

When I get stuck for words in my own native language and if I do not know how to pray about anything and everything I know that praying in other tongues helps me to say precisely what I need:

> 26. *Likewise the Spirit also helpeth our infirmities: for we know not what we should pray for as we ought: but the Spirit itself maketh intercession for us with groanings which cannot be uttered.*
> 27. *And he that searcheth the hearts knoweth what is the mind of the Spirit, because he maketh intercession for the saints according to the will of God.*
> — Romans 8:26–27

When we call out to God we know He hears our call and He always answers. He is the One God who can do that.

Chapter 2

Glory To God Everywhere

The start of my song attempts to give glory to God because the Bible tells us that God is everywhere:

> 3. *The eyes of the LORD are in every place, beholding the evil and the good.*
> — Proverbs 15:3

It is comforting to understand that God is Omnipresent; we can meet with Him anywhere, and at any time.

The words in the first verse of my song are these:

> *Glory to God in the heavens,*
> *Glory to God in the earth,*
> *Glory to God Everywhere*
>   *You Are There,*
> *Glory to God's universe.*

We are never alone. When we call out to God, He will always hear our prayers. When we need Him to help us, He is always there.

The astronomical extent of the universe is no obstacle to God. He Created everything we can see and hear and observe with all the remarkable senses He gave us.

We have eyes to detect light and shapes and colours, we have ears to hear sounds ranging from a whisper to ear-shattering noises and can discern beautiful music. We can hear the rustling of leaves on the trees and can recognise the voices of those we love.

We have a sense of touch, with which we can feel hot and cold, wet and dry, and can differentiate between rough and smooth. We can detect a gossamer breeze, and feel the gusts of wind, as we sense an impending storm.

We have a nose to help us smell fire and the fragrance of a flower, and a sense of taste that can detect sweet and sour, hot and spicy, tart and creamy, and distinguish between the herbs and spices we use to flavour our foods.

Scientists estimate the human body has over 20,000 different protein-coding genes and there could be 70,000 to 100,000 proteins in us. Where did they come from?

The possibility that even one of these proteins happens to exist by chance is exceeding remote. The probability is less than miniscule. The Word of God has this to say about any-one who has such imagined expectations:

> 1. *The fool hath said in his heart, There is no*
> *God. They are corrupt, they have done abominable*
> *works, there is none that doeth good.*
> — Psalms 14:1

We can look around us, at the earth and the sky, the mountains and the plains, the rivers, the lakes and the oceans.

Look again, at the trees and shrubs and other plants, the grasslands and the deserts. Look closer at the animal life, the bird life, the fishes, the insects and beyond.

All these features and entities get found in varying degree across most of the surface of planet Earth; a place we share with billions of other people, all, whom God has created.

When we look up into the star-studded night sky, or gaze through optical and radio telescopes, we can see more and more of His amazing universe.

> 21. *Have ye not known? have ye not heard? hath it not been told you from the beginning? have ye not understood from the foundations of the earth?* 22. *It is he that sitteth upon the circle of the earth, and the inhabitants thereof are as grasshoppers; that stretcheth out the heavens as a curtain, and spreadeth them out as a tent to dwell in:*
> — Isaiah 40:21–22

Science estimates there is over 100 billion galaxies out there and estimates there is over 100 billion *stars* in our own galaxy, the Milky Way. Do the math.

> 1. *The heavens declare the glory of God; and the firmament sheweth his handywork.*
> — Psalms 19:1

When we peer into the realms of electron microscopy and nuclear physics, we can observe the minute, intricate scale, upon which everything appears to get built. What do we know for certain?

> 19. *Where is the way where light dwelleth? and as for darkness, where is the place thereof,*
>
> . . .
>
> 24. *By what way is the light parted, . . .*
> — Job 38:19 and 24

God, our Creator is the ultimate Scientist, and He is the most magnificent Designer. As an Artisan, the work of His hands, and His palette of colours, is without compare.

With our own God given abilities, after hundreds and thousands of years of investigation, we are beginning to understand how great and how wonderful is our God.

Consider the glorious monologue spoken by God to an otherwise *"perfect and upright"* man named Job, commencing with these words:

> 1. *Then the LORD answered Job out of the whirlwind, and said,*
> 2. *Who is this that darkeneth counsel by words without knowledge?*
> 3. *Gird up now thy loins like a man; for I will demand of thee, and answer thou me.*
> 4. *Where wast thou when I laid the foundations of the earth? declare, if thou hast understanding.*
> 5. *Who hath laid the measures thereof, if thou knowest? or who hath stretched the line upon it?*
> 6. *Whereupon are the foundations thereof fastened? or who laid the corner stone thereof;*
> 7. *When the morning stars sang together, and all the sons of God shouted for joy?*
> 8. *Or who shut up the sea with doors, when it brake forth, as if it had issued out of the womb?*
> 9. *When I made the cloud the garment thereof, and thick darkness a swaddlingband for it,*
> 10. *And brake up for it my decreed place, and set bars and doors,*
> 11. *And said, Hitherto shalt thou come, but no further: and here shall thy proud waves be stayed?*
> — Job 38:1–11

I love verse 4 when God asks us *"Where were you?"*

22

Can you imagine standing there to experience the delightful scene described in verse seven?

Four chapters later, Job gets to respond to God:

> 1. *Then Job answered the LORD, and said,*
> 2. *I know that thou canst do every thing, and that no thought can be withholden from thee.*
> 3. *Who is he that hideth counsel without knowledge? therefore have I uttered that I understood not; things too wonderful for me, which I knew not.*
> 4. *Hear, I beseech thee, and I will speak: I will demand of thee, and declare thou unto me.*
> 5. *I have heard of thee by the hearing of the ear: but now mine eye seeth thee.*
> 6. *Wherefore I abhor myself, and repent in dust and ashes.*
> — Job 42:1–6

When we begin the path for our own repentance and start to recognise the greatness of God we can commence our entrance into a close and personal relationship with God.

God did not form us and create each one of us for no good reason. God wants to have a close relationship with all of His Creation; He loves what He has created.

At least six times in Genesis chapter 1, we find God saying, of His Creative work: *"it was good."*

See Genesis chapter 1, and the verses 4, 10, 12, 18, 21 and 25.

Because God created everything, He knows everything there is to know, and He instructs us to operate in a certain manner:

> 15. *And the LORD God took the man, and put*

him into the garden of Eden to dress it and to
keep it.
16. And the LORD God commanded the man,
saying, Of every tree of the garden thou mayest
freely eat:
17. But of the tree of the knowledge of good and
evil, thou shalt not eat of it: for in the day that
thou eatest thereof thou shalt surely die.
— Genesis 2:15–17

God's wholesome advice is certain to be for our own good. If you have read the book of Genesis, you will be aware of the consequence of not taking God at His Word.

What God says to us stands for eternity. What we think and imagine is not necessarily so.

God created us with intelligent brains and also the free will to choose to acknowledge Him, and to do what He says.

The alternative is for us to turn our back on Him, and suffer the consequences. It's our choice.

Almighty God loves us with a love that we can scarce comprehend.

He wants us to return the same kind of unconditional love towards Him.

He does not want a family of robots, programmed and forced to display an artificial form of affection. He wants us to be like Him, and He has provided a way whereby we can get adopted into His family.

If we are sincere in our approach to God, then it will not be long before we also, will get given the right, to call Him our heavenly Father:

14. For as many as are led by the Spirit of God,
they are the sons of God.

15. *For ye have not received the spirit of bondage again to fear; but ye have received the Spirit of adoption, whereby we cry, Abba, Father.*
— Romans 8:14–15

Consider these words that Moses spoke to the children of Israel before they were about to cross the river Jordan, and go into their *"promised land:"*

15. *See, I have set before thee this day life and good, and death and evil;*
16. *In that I command thee this day to love the LORD thy God, to walk in his ways, and to keep his commandments and his statutes and his judgments, that thou mayest live and multiply: and the LORD thy God shall bless thee in the land whither thou goest to possess it.*
17. *But if thine heart turn away, so that thou wilt not hear, but shalt be drawn away, and worship other gods, and serve them;*
18. *I denounce unto you this day, that ye shall surely perish, and that ye shall not prolong your days upon the land, whither thou passest over Jordan to go to possess it.*
19. *I call heaven and earth to record this day against you, that I have set before you life and death, blessing and cursing: therefore choose life, that both thou and thy seed may live:*
20. *That thou mayest love the LORD thy God, and that thou mayest obey his voice, and that thou mayest cleave unto him: for he is thy life, and the length of thy days: that thou mayest dwell in the land which the LORD sware unto thy fathers, to Abraham, to Isaac, and to Jacob, to give them.*
— Deuteronomy 30:15–20

God does not play games about life and death matters.

We need to take Him at His Word and do everything He commands and recommends that we must needs do. Moses implores us to *"choose life!"*

We need to recognise Almighty God's ultimate authority and give Him all the praise and the glory for the extent of His wonderful creation, both now, and for ever more.

The opening words in my song became these:

> *Glory to God in the heavens,*
> *Glory to God in the earth,*
> *Glory to God Everywhere*
>   *You Are There,*
> *Glory to God's universe.*

Chapter 3

Praise God Almighty

The second verse of this song attempts to describe why it is that we give continual praise to our God.

I know my words are woeful, inadequate and lacking at every turn. I am thankful that God remembers who we are:

> 13. *Like as a father pitieth his children, so the LORD pitieth them that fear him.*
> 14. *For he knoweth our frame; he remembereth that we are dust.*
> — Psalms 103:13–14

The Hebrew word translated as *"fear"* in verse 13 means a *"reverent fear"* or an exceeding *"great respect"* for God.

One of the first references to the Almighty nature of God is found in Genesis chapter 17:

> 1. *And when Abram was ninety years old and nine, the LORD appeared to Abram, and said unto him, I am the Almighty God; walk before me, and be thou perfect.*
> — Genesis 17:1

The Bible declares that God is One God:

> 39. *Know therefore this day, and consider it in thine heart, that the LORD he is God in heaven above, and upon the earth beneath: there is none else.*
> — Deuteronomy 4:39

There is no other God besides Him:

> 5. *I am the LORD, and there is none else, there is no God beside me: I girded thee, though thou hast not known me:*
> 6. *That they may know from the rising of the sun, and from the west, that there is none beside me. I am the LORD, and there is none else.*
> — Isaiah 45:5–6

Our repentance (change of thinking), and conversion from uncertain, or unbeliever, to absolute belief in God enables our sins (separation from God) to be *"blotted out:"* We must be willing to change.

> 19. *Repent ye therefore, and be converted, that your sins may be blotted out, when the times of refreshing shall come from the presence of the Lord.*
> — Acts 3:19

We get reminded throughout the Bible, that our salvation is not given because of anything that we do. Rather, it's through the grace and mercy of God, and is made available through the actions of Jesus Christ our Saviour:

> 5. *Not by works of righteousness which we have done, but according to his mercy he saved us, by*

the washing of regeneration, and renewing of the Holy Ghost;

6. Which he shed on us abundantly through Jesus Christ our Saviour;

7. That being justified by his grace, we should be made heirs according to the hope of eternal life.
— Titus 3:5–7

Look again at that last verse. We *"being justified by His grace"* are *"made heirs"* expecting to inherit *"the hope of eternal life."*

Consider the reasons why we praise God. He is Almighty God. He is the One True God. He gave His own Son, Jesus Christ to be the perfect sacrifice for the sins of all humanity. He has made a way for us to live together with Them throughout the rest of eternity.

The outpouring of God's Spirit upon all flesh through what Jesus called *"the promise of the Father"* is the most precious information the world affords — all because Jesus Christ chose to be obedient to God's will:

39. And he came out, and went, as he was wont, to the mount of Olives; and his disciples also followed him.

40. And when he was at the place, he said unto them, Pray that ye enter not into temptation.

41. And he was withdrawn from them about a stone's cast, and kneeled down, and prayed,

42. Saying, Father, if thou be willing, remove this cup from me: nevertheless not my will, but thine, be done.

43. And there appeared an angel unto him from heaven, strengthening him.

44. And being in an agony he prayed more earnestly: and his sweat was as it were great drops of blood falling down to the ground.

It is difficult for us to understand the perfection of God and the reasons why God's own Son, Jesus Christ, needed to die in our place.

We give great praise and thanks to Jesus Christ for enduring such torment and we give praises to God for enabling Him to carry that through.

All we need to do is be humble enough to accept His gracious gift. The entry requirements are not so onerous. *"Repent, and be baptized every one of you in the name of Jesus Christ for the remission of sins."*

The necessity for our *"repentance"* can be a hurdle for some.

There are people who have lived in honest and circumspect ways for all their life. No doubt, all they need to do is turn to God and make the request to receive His gift of the Holy Spirit, where upon they will likewise *speak in other tongues*.

There is much that the Holy Spirit experience will impart to the wisdom and understanding of every person.

Consider again the words Jesus used when He spoke to Nicodemus. He now says to all of us:

> 3. *Jesus answered and said unto him, Verily, verily, I say unto thee, Except a man be born again, he cannot see the kingdom of God.*
> . . .
> 5. *Jesus answered, Verily, verily, I say unto thee, Except a man be born of water and of the Spirit, he cannot enter into the kingdom of God.*
> 6. *That which is born of the flesh is flesh; and that which is born of the Spirit is spirit.*
> 7. *Marvel not that I said unto thee, Ye must be born again.*

In verse 3, in place of the words *"cannot see"* try substituting the phrase *"cannot fully comprehend."*

This *"born again"* process is mandatory.

It does not matter how good we think we are.

Here is what God's Word says:

> 23. *For all have sinned, and come short of the glory of God;*
> — Romans 3:23

In our natural human state we fall short of what God expects of us.

For those of us who were less than circumspect in all our ways, we need to make a more humble approach to God. Like me, our behaviour and thinking may need to go through a transformation, or two, before we become acceptable to God.

The Bible encourages us with these words:

> 9. *And I say unto you, Ask, and it shall be given you; seek, and ye shall find; knock, and it shall be opened unto you.*
> 10. *For every one that asketh receiveth; and he that seeketh findeth; and to him that knocketh it shall be opened.*
> 11. *If a son shall ask bread of any of you that is a father, will he give him a stone? or if he ask a fish, will he for a fish give him a serpent?*
> 12. *Or if he shall ask an egg, will he offer him a scorpion?*
> 13. *If ye then, being evil, know how to give good gifts unto your children: how much more shall*

your heavenly Father give the Holy Spirit to them
that ask him?
— Luke 11:9–13

Never give up. Talk to other Spirit-filled people about their experience, and what it took for them to receive the gift of the Holy Spirit, with the tangible, audible to everyone, evidence of *"speaking in other tongues."*

You should settle for nothing less than the experience Jesus called being *"born again."* Nothing less than the experience that more than 3,000 people received on the day of Pentecost, almost 2,000 years ago.

Nothing has changed. The Word of God contains lots of perfect advice and encouragement like verse 8 in the following:

> 5. *Let your conversation be without covetousness;*
> *and be content with such things as ye have: for he*
> *hath said, I will never leave thee, nor forsake thee.*
> 6. *So that we may boldly say, The Lord is my*
> *helper, and I will not fear what man shall do unto*
> *me.*
> 7. *Remember them which have the rule over you,*
> *who have spoken unto you the word of God: whose*
> *faith follow, considering the end of their conversa-*
> *tion.*
> 8. *Jesus Christ the same yesterday, and to day,*
> *and for ever.*
> — Hebrews 13:5–8

The fact that Jesus Christ is *"the same yesterday, and to day, and for ever,"* means we can take hold of what He has said and apply the same expectations for our own life, today.

If we have not yet experienced the same results, we must search our thinking. Are we trying to look good on the outside, yet still harbouring hatred, deceit or disbelief on the inside? God knows everything. Even our own personal thoughts.

After his interaction with Almighty God, the Bible character named Job knew this:

> 2. *I know that thou canst do every thing, and that no thought can be withholden from thee.*
> — Job 42:2

If we want what God has to offer we must *"come clean"* with God by owning up to the times when we know our behaviour is less than perfect and allow God to reveal other points that need our attention.

Listening to Bible talks and reading the scriptures for ourselves can help to speed up the process. We need to get baptised with the Holy Ghost like Jesus explained in Acts chapter 1 verse 5.

Remember Jesus says we: *"must be born again."*

Jesus expects nothing less from us:

> 46. *And why call ye me, Lord, Lord, and do not the things which I say?*
> — Luke 6:46

We must do what Jesus commanded.

Over time the second verse in my simple song of praises to God has morphed into these words:

> *We praise You because*
> *You're Almighty,*
> *We praise You because*

You're The One,
We praise You because You
have saved us from sin,
By the sacrifice of Your own Son.

Chapter 4

God Whom We Worship

In my short sighted, narrow minded sense of appreciation, the God Whom we worship has a multiplicity of glorious characterisations.

The Bible tells us that: *"God is great, and we know him not."*

These days most people carry a smartphone everywhere. We can install a small *"App"* that contains the complete Bible — The Word of God — so we can read and learn what God says.

Find out how to use the Navigation and Search buttons.

Look at the first two verses of the first Psalm:

> 1. *Blessed is the man that walketh not in the*
> *counsel of the ungodly, nor standeth in the way*
> *of sinners, nor sitteth in the seat of the scornful.*
> 2. *But his delight is in the law of the LORD; and*
> *in his law doth he meditate day and night.*
> — Psalms 1:1–2

Instead of walking in the ungodly ways of the world we need to delight ourself in the action of taking time to meditate in God's Law — reading and taking notice of God's Word whenever we can.

Search the scriptures.

We find verses that tell us *"God is gracious and merciful."*

"God is with us."

"God is greater than man."

"God is mighty, and despiseth not any."

"God is faithful."

"God is not the God of the dead, but of the living."

"God is our refuge and strength, a very present help in trouble."

"The foolishness of God is wiser than men."

"The weakness of God is stronger than men."

"God is light, and in him is no darkness at all."

"God is a consuming fire."

John the Baptist had these words to say:

> 11. *I indeed baptize you with water unto repentance. but he that cometh after me is mightier than I, whose shoes I am not worthy to bear: he shall baptize you with the Holy Ghost, and with fire:*
> 12. *Whose fan is in his hand, and he will throughly purge his floor, and gather his wheat into the garner; but he will burn up the chaff with unquenchable fire.*
> — Matthew 3:11–12

This likens us to a grain of wheat gathered together into a place of storage. Our rough edges, the chaff, gets rubbed off and then thoroughly destroyed through the unquenchable fire of the Holy Spirit. All that remains is the precious grain of wheat — the real us.

"Every word of God is pure."

"God is not the author of confusion."

"God is no respecter of persons."

"God is true."

"God is love."

"God is a Spirit."

In the book of Galatians we can read about the nine delightful characteristics called the *"fruit of the Spirit:"*

> 22. *But the fruit of the Spirit is love, joy, peace, longsuffering, gentleness, goodness, faith,*
> 23. *Meekness, temperance: against such there is no law.*
> — Galatians 5:22–23

God exhibits all these and He gives each of them to us as part of the gift when we receive His Holy Spirit.

These nine behavioural qualities become part of our new persona imparted by that precious *"promise of the Father."*

God is the Creator of heaven and earth. His Righteous Son, Jesus Christ, is Saviour of the world and the Holy Spirit that God has made available to all provides us with direction and understanding we never knew before.

He is God the Father. He is God the Son. He is God the Holy Spirit.

As a starting point I praise and worship all three *"just as One."*

The vital roles They each play in our Salvation — our return to the heavenly Father — is not discounted on any front.

The words I found for my third verse are these:

> *We worship the God of Creation,*
> *We worship the Saviour*
>   *Your Son, Jesus Christ,*
> *We worship the Spirit*
>   *You poured out on us,*
> *And we worship all Three*
>   *just as One.*

At the start of the Bible book of Genesis we read the following words of introduction to our God:

> 1. *In the beginning God created the heaven and the earth.*
> 2. *And the earth was without form, and void; and darkness was upon the face of the deep. And the Spirit of God moved upon the face of the waters.*
> 3. *And God said, Let there be light: and there was light.*
> 4. *And God saw the light, that it was good: and God divided the light from the darkness.*
> 5. *And God called the light Day, and the darkness he called Night. And the evening and the morning were the first day.*
> — Genesis 1:1–5

In the New Testament gospel of John, we read these words:

> 1. *In the beginning was the Word, and the Word was with God, and the Word was God.*
> 2. *The same was in the beginning with God.*

3. All things were made by him; and without him was not any thing made that was made.
4. In him was life; and the life was the light of men.
5. And the light shineth in darkness; and the darkness comprehended it not.
— John 1:1–5

In the last book of Revelation, in our Bibles we read:

8. I am Alpha and Omega, the beginning and the ending, saith the Lord, which is, and which was, and which is to come, the Almighty.
— Revelation 1:8

With certainty there is a lot to learn about the wonderful God of Creation and His Son Jesus Christ and the Holy Spirit Who mediates between us.

Our appreciation of all His ways begins to grow as the Spirit of God reveals ever more and more.

We have received what Jesus calls *"the promise of the Father."*

This free gift from God is always accompanied by the ability to speak out in other *unlearned* tongues.

This ability is given at the instant in which God's Holy Spirit enters into our own mortal being and makes us one again with the Father and the Son and the Holy Spirit.

Jesus calls this experience being *"baptized with the Holy Ghost."*

This miracle gift from God helps us to become more like Jesus.

When Jesus came to the banks of the Jordan, to get baptized by John the Baptist we read:

39

16. And Jesus, when he was baptized, went up straightway out of the water: and, lo, the heavens were opened unto him, and he saw the Spirit of God descending like a dove, and lighting upon him:

17. And lo a voice from heaven, saying, This is my beloved Son, in whom I am well pleased.
— Matthew 3:16–17

Notice that John the Baptist observed: *"the Spirit of God descending like a dove, and lighting upon him."*

Jesus got born into a flesh and blood body like we do.

When He got baptized the Holy Spirit descended upon Him.

For Jesus this was straightway possible because unlike us, we read He was *"without sin."*

14. Seeing then that we have a great high priest, that is passed into the heavens, Jesus the Son of God, let us hold fast our profession.

15. For we have not an high priest which cannot be touched with the feeling of our infirmities; but was in all points tempted like as we are, yet without sin.

16. Let us therefore come boldly unto the throne of grace, that we may obtain mercy, and find grace to help in time of need.
— Hebrews 4:14–16

We need to make a personal repentant approach to God. This could take time to get right. God will help us to sort out what we need to do.

When we receive the *"promise of the Father"* we receive the precious Holy Spirit from God.

In Acts chapter 2 verse 4 we read:

*4. And they were all filled with the Holy Ghost,
and began to speak with other tongues, as the
Spirit gave them utterance.*
— Acts 2:4

The empty place we had inside is now *"filled"* with the Holy
Spirit.

Believe with all your heart there is no place left for any of
our old ungodly ways of thinking.

From that moment on we can call Jesus *"Lord"* and can get
to know Him like a brother. From that moment on we can
can get to know God as our *"heavenly Father."*

Jesus Christ promises that He and the heavenly Father will
have come and made their *"abode"* with us:

*23. Jesus answered and said unto him, If a man
love me, he will keep my words: and my Father
will love him, and we will come unto him, and
make our abode with him.*
— John 14:23

We find God is a miracle working God. He is a healing God
and He provides for our every need — not our inconsiderate
wants or demands.

On occasion when we pray to God we could find His answer
to us is *"No"* or *"Not yet"* or *"Not in that way."*

We could need to reconsider our ways:

*3. Ye ask, and receive not, because ye ask amiss,
that ye may consume it upon your lusts.*
— James 4:3

God is well aware:

9. The heart is deceitful above all things, and des-
perately wicked: who can know it?
10. I the LORD search the heart, I try the reins,
even to give every man according to his ways, and
according to the fruit of his doings.
— Jeremiah 17:9–10

As we look around the world today through the eyes of nightly news broadcasts we observe the increase of atrocity, calamity, corruption, despair, destruction, hatred, inhuman-ity, ruthlessness, savagery, terrorism, vandalism, violence, and we see wars and rumours of war. Mankind continues to grow desperately wicked.

The next verses from the book of Galatians *precede* those we have already seen, that described the miraculous *"fruit of God's Holy Spirit."*

These verses outline a list of the types of behaviours we need to *leave behind* us and never consider doing again:

19. Now the works of the flesh are manifest, which
are these; Adultery, fornication, uncleanness, las-
civiousness,
20. Idolatry, witchcraft, hatred, variance, emula-
tions, wrath, strife, seditions, heresies,
21. Envyings, murders, drunkenness, revellings,
and such like: of the which I tell you before, as I
have also told you in time past, that they which do
such things shall not inherit the kingdom of God.
— Galatians 5:19–21

Our God is more glorious than these worldly elements of be-haviour.

We must never think about acting in any of these ways again. Be quick. Step away with haste. Learn to say *"No."* It does not hurt.

God has created us with the potential to overcome that side of our human nature. The missing ingredient gets provided when we accept God's gift of the Holy Spirit.

Without the Holy Spirit, we are always trying to do everything on our own. In our own strength we will always fail.

Look at this description of reality and consider verse 14:

> 9. *But as it is written, Eye hath not seen, nor ear heard, neither have entered into the heart of man, the things which God hath prepared for them that love him.*
> 10. *But God hath revealed them unto us by his Spirit: for the Spirit searcheth all things, yea, the deep things of God.*
> 11. *For what man knoweth the things of a man, save the spirit of man which is in him? even so the things of God knoweth no man, but the Spirit of God.*
> 12. *Now we have received, not the spirit of the world, but the spirit which is of God; that we might know the things that are freely given to us of God.*
> 13. *Which things also we speak, not in the words which man's wisdom teacheth, but which the Holy Ghost teacheth; comparing spiritual things with spiritual.*
> 14. *But the natural man receiveth not the things of the Spirit of God: for they are foolishness unto him: neither can he know them, because they are spiritually discerned.*
> — 1 Corinthians 2:9–14

If anything I am saying (writing here) seems to be impossible to understand, please know and believe that other people, myself included, encounter the same overwhelming feeling from TMI (Too Much Information).

The key to coming to grips with what God says to us is to understand what Jesus said: *"You must be born again."*

The way we get *"born again"* is to follow the advice Peter gave on the day of Pentecost:

> 38. *Then Peter said unto them, Repent, and be baptized every one of you in the name of Jesus Christ for the remission of sins, and ye shall receive the gift of the Holy Ghost.*
> 39. *For the promise is unto you, and to your children, and to all that are afar off, even as many as the LORD our God shall call.*
> — Acts 2:38–39

When we *"repent"* with our whole heart then God responds and fills us with His *"gift of the Holy Spirit"* and we will *"speak in other tongues."*

From that point onwards everything we read in the Bible (God's Word) will begin to make more sense and no doubt we will observe that what God says applies directly to us.

God's words will be talking to us and about our experience.

The indwelling presence of the heavenly Father and His Son Jesus Christ provided through the Holy Spirit will bring us the ability to discern the truth and will give us the strength to leave our old life behind.

The words in the third verse of my song became:

> *We worship the God of Creation,*
> *We worship the Saviour*
> *   Your Son, Jesus Christ,*
> *We worship the Spirit*
> *   You poured out on us,*
> *And we worship all Three*
> *   just as One.*

Chapter 5

God Is Merciful To Us

Walking on, as a Spirit filled son or daughter of the living God, enables us to begin to appreciate how much God cares for us, and we begin to see how He provides for us.

We begin to appreciate glorious words we find in the Bible such as these:

> 1. *Make a joyful noise unto the LORD, all ye lands.*
> 2. *Serve the LORD with gladness: come before his presence with singing.*
> 3. *Know ye that the LORD he is God: it is he that hath made us, and not we ourselves; we are his people, and the sheep of his pasture.*
> 4. *Enter into his gates with thanksgiving, and into his courts with praise: be thankful unto him, and bless his name.*
> 5. *For the LORD is good; his mercy is everlasting; and his truth endureth to all generations.*
> — Psalms 100:1–5

Look at the delightful words in verse 5.

"For the LORD is good; his mercy is everlasting; and his truth endureth to all generations."

Take these words to heart. Believe them. I believe these are true beyond any shadow of doubt.

At times, in the meetings of the church I attend, we will sing the words of a single verse from the book of Micah:

> 8. *He hath shewed thee, O man, what is good; and what doth the LORD require of thee, but to do justly, and to love mercy, and to walk humbly with thy God?*
> — Micah 6:8

This is a beautiful précis of what God expects of us. Instead of taking our cues from television shows and horror movies, we can take our leading and guidance directly from the gift of God's Holy Spirit.

Instead of taking no concern for others, we consider justice and pray for their deliverance.

Instead of indifference we learn to show mercy.

Instead of riding on our own high horse we can step down and show humility. Try walking in another person's shoes. Witness to them about the grace and mercy of God.

When Jesus Christ walked with His disciples, He performed wonderful miracles of healing and provision for those who would believe:

> 14. *And Jesus went forth, and saw a great multitude, and was moved with compassion toward them, and he healed their sick.*
> — Matthew 14:14

We read earlier:

8. *Jesus Christ the same yesterday, and to day,*
and for ever.
— Hebrews 13:8

We can call out all the more to God and to Jesus Christ, to heal and to provide for the needs of us and those around us today.

God greatly cares for and loves His entire Creation. We are a special part of that because we have the ability to communicate with Him in Spirit and in truth.

Consider these words from the book of 1st Peter:

6. *Humble yourselves therefore under the mighty*
hand of God, that he may exalt you in due time:
7. *Casting all your care upon him; for he careth*
for you.
— 1 Peter 5:6–7

God does care for us. He loves us. He has granted us access to *"the throne of grace:"*

16. *Let us therefore come boldly unto the throne of*
grace, that we may obtain mercy, and find grace to
help in time of need.
— Hebrews 4:16

The Psalmist knew God would answer his call:

6. *Give ear, O LORD, unto my prayer; and at-*
tend to the voice of my supplications.
7. *In the day of my trouble I will call upon thee:*
for thou wilt answer me.
8. *Among the gods there is none like unto thee,*
O Lord; neither are there any works like unto thy
works.

9. *All nations whom thou hast made shall come and worship before thee, O Lord; and shall glorify thy name.*
10. *For thou art great, and doest wondrous things: thou art God alone.*
11. *Teach me thy way, O LORD; I will walk in thy truth: unite my heart to fear thy name.*
12. *I will praise thee, O Lord my God, with all my heart: and I will glorify thy name for evermore.*
13. *For great is thy mercy toward me: and thou hast delivered my soul from the lowest hell.*
— Psalms 86:6–13

Look at verses 7 and 10 and 13. No wonder he says: "*I will praise thee, O Lord my God, with all my heart: and I will glorify thy name for evermore.*"

Consider the words in this most beautiful of Psalms:

1. *He that dwelleth in the secret place of the most High shall abide under the shadow of the Almighty.*
2. *I will say of the LORD, He is my refuge and my fortress: my God; in him will I trust.*
3. *Surely he shall deliver thee from the snare of the fowler, and from the noisome pestilence.*
4. *He shall cover thee with his feathers, and under his wings shalt thou trust: his truth shall be thy shield and buckler.*
5. *Thou shalt not be afraid for the terror by night; nor for the arrow that flieth by day;*
6. *Nor for the pestilence that walketh in darkness; nor for the destruction that wasteth at noonday.*
7. *A thousand shall fall at thy side, and ten thousand at thy right hand; but it shall not come nigh thee.*

8. *Only with thine eyes shalt thou behold and see the reward of the wicked.*

9. *Because thou hast made the LORD, which is my refuge, even the most High, thy habitation;*

10. *There shall no evil befall thee, neither shall any plague come nigh thy dwelling.*

11. *For he shall give his angels charge over thee, to keep thee in all thy ways.*

12. *They shall bear thee up in their hands, lest thou dash thy foot against a stone.*

13. *Thou shalt tread upon the lion and adder: the young lion and the dragon shalt thou trample under feet.*

14. *Because he hath set his love upon me, therefore will I deliver him: I will set him on high, because he hath known my name.*

15. *He shall call upon me, and I will answer him: I will be with him in trouble; I will deliver him, and honour him.*

16. *With long life will I satisfy him, and shew him my salvation.*

— Psalms 91:1–16

I love to saturate myself in the words of each verse. Their contemplation brings me great comfort and peace and joy.

Consider these words proclaimed by The Lord up on mount Sinai when Moses met with the Lord God there:

5. *And the LORD descended in the cloud, and stood with him there, and proclaimed the name of the LORD.*

6. *And the LORD passed by before him, and proclaimed, The LORD, The LORD God, merciful and gracious, longsuffering, and abundant in goodness and truth,*

— Exodus 34:5–6

God is *"merciful and gracious."*

God is *"longsuffering"* toward us.

God is *"abundant in goodness and truth."*

The inadequate words of the final verse in my song came to be these. Their one saving grace — I sing them with faith and belief:

> *You care for and You heal*
> *   all we pray for,*
> *You distribute Your Mercy*
> *   and everlasting Grace,*
> *You broadcast Your Love*
> *   overflowing on us,*
> *And protect us*
> *   within Your embrace.*

Chapter 6

A Melody

Settling on a suitable melody to sing the words of my song *"Glory To God Everywhere You are There"* took me a while to resolve in my mind.

My song writing has always been somewhat haphazard. I could be changing between two or three chords on my guitar then sing three or four words to give me a phrase in the rhythm I am strumming.

I tend to play that over and over and over again for a long time until it sounds the way I like. The words reflect the thoughts and contemplations coming across my mind as I play.

After my Ischaemic Stroke it took quite some time before I could again pick up a guitar and hold up the neck to where I could correctly finger a chord and practice ways to strum the guitar as I wanted.

I spend hours sitting at my Linux computer every day, writing my books, writing and testing computer script programs and playing and refining music snippets.

After a little investigation I turned to using a clever and most capable music notation system called: *"Lilypond."*

Please visit their web page for more details:

`https://lilypond.org`

LilyPond is free software and part of the GNU Project. It's published under the GNU General Public License.

The Lilypond system will run on Linux or Windows or Apple PCs and there is a GUI front end called "`frescobaldi`" to help make text input and music output easier.

Unlike expensive graphical score editing systems, Lilypond presents a compiled symbolic language system that uses a plain text file describing the music elements.

The note names, note pitch, note duration and other music articulation information gets defined with the use of plain text characters and numbers and symbols.

It's not as difficult as that may sound. If you use a computer and can find a plain text editor program (not a word processor application) then you are set to go after you find and install the Lilypond software.

When initially installed the Lilypond system uses lower-case letters 'a' through 'g' for the note names and uses the addition of '`es`' to flatten a note, or '`is`' to sharpen a note. For example: '`ees`' is a flattened E note, and '`fis`' is a sharpened F note.

Although I do not sight read music (the dots and squiggles on a page), I knew where to find the notes I wanted on the fret board of my guitar.

I began to pick those out, slowly, letting my ear discern the note pitches I wanted and writing down the note names as I went.

Next I needed to determine the note lengths in the 6/8 timing I had chosen. It was a slow process at first.

After a single or three-character note name, we can append one or more right single quote (') characters to *raise* the note by an *octave*. Or we can add one or more comma (,) characters to *lower* the note by an *octave*.

The duration for a note gets specified by appending a small integer, like '2' for a half note (a *minim*), '4' for a quarter note (a *crotchet*), '8' for an eighth note (a *quaver*), or '16' for a sixteenth note (a *semi-quaver*), etc.

A dotted note gets indicated with one or more dot ('.') characters appended after that.

For example writing the three characters:

```
d4.
```

defines a 'd' note to get sounded as a dotted quarter note.

I think the keyboard interaction helped me with manual dexterity recovery, and the programming side helped me with brain capacity recovery.

The second and subsequent notes of a sequence of notes of *equal* length do not need a duration number until that note length needs to change. For example:

```
a'8 a' a' b' a' g' a' d'2 r8
```

This produces seven *eighth* notes, and a *half* note, followed by an *eighth* rest. Two bars in my 6/8 music.

A rest (the absence of sound) gets specified by the letter 'r' with a duration number appended.

A tuplet of notes, for example, three notes played in the time of two, or five notes played in the time of four, gets written like this:

```
\times 4/5 { d'8 e'8 fis'8 g'8 a'8 }
```

Other music elements like the *"tie"* or the *"slur"* get specified with a tilde (˜) character between two notes that need to get tied to produce a longer duration:

```
c2˜ c4
```

A pair of parentheses '(' and ')' characters get used to show a *"slur"* across two or more notes of different pitch:

```
c( a)
```

There is other notation markup such as '<' and '>' to enclose the notes of a chord:

```
< c e g >4
```

Where you see pairs of angle brackets like '<<' and '>>' these enclose parallel sections of music using separate staves or clefs.

You can select the appropriate Clef for your music with entries like:

```
\clef "treble"  \clef "bass"
```

Other clefs include:

```
\clef "tenor"    \clef "treble_8"
```

Specify the Time Signature with:

```
\time 3/4  \time 4/4  \time 6/8
```

Set the Key for a piece with:

```
\key c \major   \key d \minor
```

The Lilypond markup language permits the user to define *variables* for reuse within a piece of music:

```
var = { ... }
```

and down further we can use:

```
\var \var
```

to sound and repeat the music that got defined between the two curly brace characters '{' and '}'.

There are elements to define a '\scrore { ... }' and the score *layout* with '\layout { ... }' and there is a request to produce MIDI output with '\midi { }' and other items like headings and lyrics.

The percent character ('%') commences a line of comment text.

Here is the Lilypond source file I produced to help me determine the melody for my song:

```
1  %
2  % Program:
3  %   g22g.ly --> Lilypond music source code
4  %
5  % Author:
6  %   Lawson Hanson, 20150307 and 20250415.
7  %
8  % Purpose:
9  %   A Lilypond input source file for a composition
10 %   called "Glory to God Everywhere You Are There"
11 %   a song of praises to God written by the author.
12 %
13 \version "2.20.0"
14 #(set-default-paper-size "a4")
```

```
15  #(set-global-staff-size 24 )
16  \header{
17    title = "Glory to God Everywhere You are There"
18    composer = "Lawson Hanson"
19    arranger = \markup { "5-March-2015." }
20    tagline = #ff
21    copyright = "Copyright (C) Lawson I. Hanson 2015.
22                        All rights reserved."
23  }
24
25  melody = {
26    a'8 a' a' b' a' g' a' d'2 r8
27    a'8 a' a' b' a' g' a'2.
28    b'8 b' b' cis''4 b'16 cis''16 d''8 a'8 g' fis'4.
29    fis'8 fis' fis' g' fis' e' d'2 r4
30  }
31
32  guitar = {
33    \chordmode {
34      d4. g4. | d2.     | d4. g4. | d2. |
35      g4. a4. | d4. d4. | d4. g4. | d2.
36    }
37  }
38
39  second = {
40    a'8 d' a' b' a' g' a' d'4. d'16 e' fis' g'
41    a'8 d' a' b' a' g' a'4
42      \times 4/5 { d'8 e'8 fis'8 g'8 a'8 }
43    b'8 b' b' cis''4 b'16 cis''16 d''8 a'8 g' fis'4.
44    fis'8 e' fis' g' fis' e' d'2 r4
45  }
46
47  third = {
48    a8 d a b a g a d4. d16 e fis g
49    a8 d a b a g a8 d8 e8 fis8 g8 a8
50    b8 b b cis'4 b16 cis'16 d'8 a8 g fis4.
51    fis8 e fis g fis e d2 r4
52  }
53
54  other = {
55    a8 a a b a g a d2 r8
56    a8 a a b a g a2.
57    b8 b b cis'4 cis'8 d'8 a8 g fis4.
58    fis8 fis fis g fis e d2 r4
59  }
60
61  \score {
62    {
63      \tempo 8 = 132
64      \numericTimeSignature
65      \time 6/8
66      \key d \major
67      \clef treble
68
69      \repeat volta 4 {
70      <<
```

```
 71     {
 72        \melody
 73        \addlyrics {
 74          % \set stanza = #1. "
 75          Glo -- ry to God
 76            in the heav -- ens,
 77          Glo -- ry to God
 78            in the earth,
 79          Glo -- ry to God Eve -- ry
 80            where, You are There,
 81          Glo -- ry to God's
 82            u -- ni -- verse.
 83        }
 84     }
 85     \new Staff {
 86        \key d \major
 87        \clef treble
 88
 89        <<
 90          \context ChordNames \guitar
 91          \context Staff \guitar
 92        >>
 93     }
 94     \new Staff {
 95        \key d \major
 96        \clef bass
 97
 98        \third
 99     }
100   >>
101    }
102 }
103 \layout {
104    textheight = 220.\mm
105    linewidth = 150.\mm
106    indent = 0.\mm
107 }
108 \midi { }
109 }
110
111 %    \wordwrap-string #"
112
113 \markup{
114   \fill-line {
115   ""
116    {
117      \column {
118        \left-align {
119          \line { . }
120          \line { Verse 2.  }
121          \line { We_praise You be -- cause
122                  You're Al -- migh -- ty, }
123          \line { We_praise You be -- cause
124                  You're The One, }
125          \line { We_praise You because You
126                  have saved us from sin, }
```

57

```
127          \line { By_the_sac -- rif -- ice
128                  of Your own Son.  }
129          \line { . }
130          \line { Verse 3.  }
131          \line { We wor -- ship the
132                  God of Cre -- a -- tion, }
133          \line { We wor -- ship the Sav -- iour,
134                  Your Son, Jesus Christ }
135          \line { We wor -- ship the Spi -- rit
136                  You poured out on us, }
137          \line { And_we wor -- ship all Three
138                  just as One.  }
139          \line { . }
140          \line { Verse 4.  }
141          \line { You_care for and You heal
142                  all we pray for, }
143          \line { You_dis -- trib -- ute Your
144                  Mer -- cy and everlasting Grace, }
145          \line { You broad -- cast Your Love,
146                  over -- flowing on us, }
147          \line { And pro -- tect us with -- in
148                  Your em -- brace.  }
149        }
150      }
151    }
152  ""
153  }
154 }
```

When I run the following Linux shell command:

```
$ lilypond g22g.ly
```

The dollar symbol ($) at the start of the line represents my shell prompt. Do not enter that character.

The 'lilypond' command compiles the plain text file named 'g22g.ly' and provided there are no errors in my code I will get two new output files:

```
g22g.midi
```

and:

```
g22g.pdf
```

The PDF file is a printable form of the music. On Linux I use the 'qpdfview' program to display the PDF file:

```
$ qpdfview g22g.pdf
```

To listen to the music, the MIDI file can get sent to a MIDI player. On Linux I use the 'timidity' program:

```
$ timidity g22g.midi
```

Here is a list of Lilypond absolute note names for a six string guitar in a standard tuning:

```
 1    #
 2    # Program:
 3    #   gtr-lyp-notes.txt
 4    #
 5    # Author:
 6    #   Lawson Hanson, 20211103.
 7    #
 8    # Purpose:
 9    #   Lilypond absolute note names for a
10    #   six-string guitar in standard tuning:
11    #
12    # Format:
13    # ------
14    #   Fret  String numbers -->
15    #   -1    6     5     4     3     2     1
16    #   0     e,    a,    d     g     b     e'
17    #   1     f,    ais,  dis   gis   c'    f'
18    #   ...
19    #   12    e,    a,    d     g     b'    e'
20    #   ...
21    #   19    b     e'    a'    d''   fis'' b''
22    #
23    # Notes (fret representations):
24    #   1. Fret '-1' the string numbers line
25    #   2. Fret '0'  the Nut (an open string)
26    #
27    -1    6     5     4     3     2     1
28    0     e,    a,    d     g     b     e'
29          ==================================
30    1     f,    ais,  dis   gis   c'    f'
31    2     fis,  b,    e     a     cis'  fis'
32    3     g,    c     f     ais   d'    g'
33          ----------------------------------
34    4     gis,  cis   fis   b     dis'  gis'
```

```
35  5    a,    d      g      c'     e'      a'
36       -------------------------------------------
37  6    ais,  dis    gis    cis'   f'      ais'
38  7    b,    e      a      d'     fis'    b'
39       -------------------------------------------
40  8    c     f      ais    dis'   g'      c''
41  9    cis   fis    b      e'     gis'    cis''
42  10   d     g      c'     f'     a'      d''
43       -------------------------------------------
44  11   dis   gis    cis'   fis'   ais'    dis''
45  12   e     a      d'     g'     b'      e''
46       -------------------------------------------
47  13   f     ais    dis'   gis'   c''     f''
48  14   fis   b      e'     a'     cis''   fis''
49  15   g     c'     f'     ais'   d''     g''
50  16   gis   cis'   fis'   b'     dis''   gis''
51  17   a     d'     g'     c''    e''     a''
52  18   ais   dis'   gis'   cis''  f''     ais''
53  19   b     e'     a'     d''    fis''   b''
54  20   c'    f'     ais'   dis''  g''     c'''
```

I find that helpful when I am trying to figure out the note name information for the notes at the fret stops I am playing.

Lilypond includes exceptionally good documentation, all available at the extensive resources found on the web page I listed near the start of this chapter.

There is introductory material with tutorials as well as more in-depth learning and reference material.

Chapter 7

The Music Score

The following image displays the musical score produced by running the 'lilypond' command to compile the plain text source file listed in the previous chapter.

Glory to God Everywhere You are There

Lawson Hanson

5-March-2015.

Glory to God in the heavens,   Glory to God in the earth,

Glory to God Every where, You are There, Glory to God's u-niverse.

Verse 2.

We_praise You be -- cause You're Al -- migh -- ty,
We_praise You be -- cause You're The One,
We_praise You because You have saved us from sin,
By_the_sac -- rif -- ice of Your own Son.

Verse 3.

We wor -- ship the God of Cre -- a -- tion,
We wor -- ship the Sav -- iour, Your Son, Jesus Christ
We wor -- ship the Spi -- rit You poured out on us,
And_we wor -- ship all Three just as One.

Verse 4.

You_care for and You heal all we pray for,
You_dis -- trib -- ute Your Mer -- cy and everlasting Grace,
You broad -- cast Your Love, over -- flowing on us,
And pro -- tect us with -- in Your em -- brace.

Chapter 8

More Music

In my younger days I played in a small band at the church I have attended for almost 50 years.

```
https://www.revivalcentres.org
```

Age and health issues have slowed me down, yet there are some examples of my music on-line.

To listen to this music you could try a YouTube™search:

```
https://www.YouTube.com/results?search_query=Lawson+Hanson+music
```

You should find a *"Remixed: Lord God Almighty,"* and other songs like: *"Faith," "He Is Lord," "On A Day Like This"* and *"Prodigal Son."*

Note: You can find sixteen (16) different songs. Each YouTube *track* has a single *still* image, not a video clip (other than the advertising they seem to display — please hit "Skip"), and each should be playable on a low bandwidth connection; i.e., will not use too much of your Internet data limit.

In an undirected Google™ search, you may need to use quotation marks around my two names because there are other people called *"Lawson,"* and a band named *"Hanson,"* none of whom are the same *"Lawson Hanson"* who resides in my skin.

Otherwise, there are two *Albums,* each of which has eight tracks. I have distributed these through DistroKid™ and people should be able to find the tracks through digital download and/or audio streaming channels such as: Amazon™, Apple Music™, Spotify™ and perhaps some others. An example of these located at Apple Music is:

- He Is Lord

  https://music.apple.com/au/album/he-is-lord/1473958665

- Prodigal Son's Return

  https://music.apple.com/au/album/prodigal-sons-return/1473966231

Or on Spotify:

- He Is Lord

  https://open.spotify.com/album/6TC5awGoyok3cXY7fU9tkl

- Prodigal Son's Return

  https://open.spotify.com/album/5RuDTHcTKAzYYoKHBe050s

Accreditations

Over the course of more than four decades I have performed my music live with the accompaniment of different musicians.

I offer my sincere thanks and great appreciation to the talented individuals who spent countless hours of their precious time in rehearsals and preparations for the performances we managed to present.

We made rough recordings of the music over the years. Accompanying my own lyrics, melodies, vocals and rhythm guitar, the recordings variously include other instrumental and vocal performances by:

By Musical Instrument

- Bass Guitar:

    - Bradley Parker-Hill
    - Mark Stanborough

- Drums:

    - Jonathon Longfield
    - Mark Stanborough
    - Nigel Picknell
    - Paul Anastassopoulos
    - Stuart Bowden

- Lead Guitar:

    - Clive Smith
    - Mark Stanborough

- Saxophone:

- – Mark Stanborough
- – Peter deMunk

- Sound Recording:

  - – Mark Stanborough

- Vocals:

  - – Paul Anastassopoulos
  - – Peter deMunk